Shekhinah
The Presence

Shekhinah
the presence

joseph zitt

photographs by matthew sharlot

the apocryphile press
BERKELEY, CA
www.apocryphile.org

apocryphile press
BERKELEY, CA

Apocryphile Press
1700 Shattuck Ave #81
Berkeley, CA 94709
www.apocryphile.org

This edition first published in 1992 by Metatron Press.
Apocryphile Press Edition, 2009.

Copyright @ 1992 by Joseph Zitt. All rights reserved. Printed in the United States of America. No part of this book may be used or reproduced in any manner whatsoever without written permission except in the case of brief quotations in critical articles or reviews.

Photographs by Matthew Sharlot.

Book design by Joseph Zitt and Eureka Purity.

Printed in the United States of America
ISBN 1-933993-71-5

In memory of
Reverend Naftali Ungar

and

For my parents

Contents

About the Shekhinah	9
TEFILLIN	
Opening	11
BIRCHOT HASHACHAR	
Morning Blessings	19
PESUKEY D'ZIMRA	
Verses of Song	29
BORCHU	
Bless the Lord	39
SHEMA	
Listen	53
AMIDAH	
Silent Prayer	71
KRIYAT HATORAH	
Reading	77
ALENU	
Our Duty	109
KADDISH	
Mourner's Prayer	131
HOSAFOT	
Beyond Conclusion	137
Afterword	149
Bibliography	153

About the Shekhinah

"*Shekhinah* is the frequently used Talmudic term denoting the visible and audible manifestation of God's presence on Earth. In its ultimate development as it appears in the late Midrash literature, the Shekhinah stood for an independent, feminine divine entity prompted by her compassionate nature to argue with God in defense of man."
—RAFAEL PATAI

"The Shekhinah is precisely that aspect of God with which we can be in relation, and it is experienced in joint study, community gatherings, lovemaking, and other moments of common and intimate human connection."
—JUDITH PLASKOW

"For some Gnostics . . . , the Shekhinah, as the last of the Sefiroth, becomes the 'daughter' who, although her home is the 'form of light,' must wander into far lands . . . . She is not only Queen, daughter and bride of God, but also the mother of every individual in Israel."
—GERSHOM G. SCHOLEM

"Therefore, before performing a mitsvah or an act of charity, one must say 'To unite the name of the Holy One, blessed be he, and his Shekhinah, in fear and love, to join YH with WH, in the name of all Israel.'"
—HAYYIM VITAL

Tefillin
תפילין
Opening

TEFILLIN
Opening

HERE at the start of the day
we who can tell
    the black thread from the blue
    the blue from the white
    the black from the white
now (when consensus takes
    the place of agreement)
stand and prepare.

•

We who have entered this sacred room
    (although, indeed, any room
    can be sanctified
    by this purpose)
have paused by the doorpost,
    touched the box of memories
    that waits there,
    silent,
    whether for us
    or for Elijah
        who will pass through all the portals
        and join the scrolls
        upon the doorposts of all our houses
        into one,
have kissed our hands,

SHEKHINAH

    as if to kiss,
    by indirection,
    the welcoming scrolls
    posted by the doors
then entered this room,
    greeted by the faint rays
    of the new morning's sun
    that cast fresh, elongated shadows
    of the Ark,
    of our books of learning,
    of our lives.
We turn to the East,
    to welcome the sun,
    and see the words
    (now hard to read
    in their contrast with the
    sharp morning rays)
    inscribed here on the Ark:

                              •

Know
Before Whom
You Stand.

                        •

Each of us,
    for the moment,
    alone,
reaches for the Talit bag
    (for some, velvet,
        the deep blue of the
        roof of the sky
        in the dying of the night

OPENING

   just before the sun
   returns to welcome us,
  for the adventurous or whimsical,
   other fabrics,
   other colors,
   expressing
   other joys or memories)
withdraws the thin shawl
  (white,
  with its stripes of black or blue
  and the fringes at its corners,
   each carefully prepared,
   each with eight threads,
    one twisted seven times
     around the other seven
     and tied
    then eight times
     and tied
    then eleven
     and tied
    and thirteen
   all these numbers
    merging with the alphabet
    in permutation
    and computations
   so every sum and product
    can somehow praise
    the Holy Name)
whispers the prayer inscribed on its margins,
wraps it around himself
over his head

SHEKHINAH

    (enclosing the wearer, for the moment,
    in a womb of wool or silk,
    in a white filtered shroud of light
        like the one seen by the soul,
        then forgotten
        in the instant before birth
        when the angels kissed it
        to seal away, for a time,
        its knowledge of heaven),
then lets it drift down to his shoulders,
    his back encased in white,
    the fringes
    resting like guardians
    about his thighs.

            •

And from another bag,
    (smaller,
    echoing in design the larger,
    as a student might deduce a principle
        in deriving similarities
        from the general
        to the particular)
small boxes, leather,
each box containing smaller skins,
    cousins to the watchman scroll
    greeted and kissed by the door,
each attached to leather straps.
One at a time,
    with care,
    with blessings,
we bind them to ourselves,

OPENING

the first sliding up the left arm
to rest by the heart,
then its straps, winding,
    as if echoing outside our bodies
    the blood that rushes life
    within our hands,
        seven turns down the forearm
        then three times around
           the middle finger
           betrothing us
                to the Holy Presence
                forever
                for righteousness
                    justice
                    kindness
                    mercy
                for the faith in
                    the faithfulness
                    of the patterns
        and around the hand
        its patterns forming letters
            of yet another version
            of another Holy Name,
the second resting between our eyes,
suspended from a loop
    that rests upon our heads
    like a crown of duty
with twin descendants
    draping from behind
    over our shoulders,
    across the shawl,

SHEKHINAH

then draping down our chests
    echoing the poise of the fringes
    that rest below.
                    •

Thus garbed,
thus prepared,
we concentrate our attention,
    open our books to the proper pages,
turn to the East
    to the Ark
    to the sun
    to the silent walls of Jerusalem,
and, somewhat together
    somewhat alone
    each, in his separate intent,
    strengthened
        by the others gathered there,
                    •

we begin
                    •

in hushes close to silence
to pray.

Birchot Hashachar
ברכות השחר
Morning Blessings

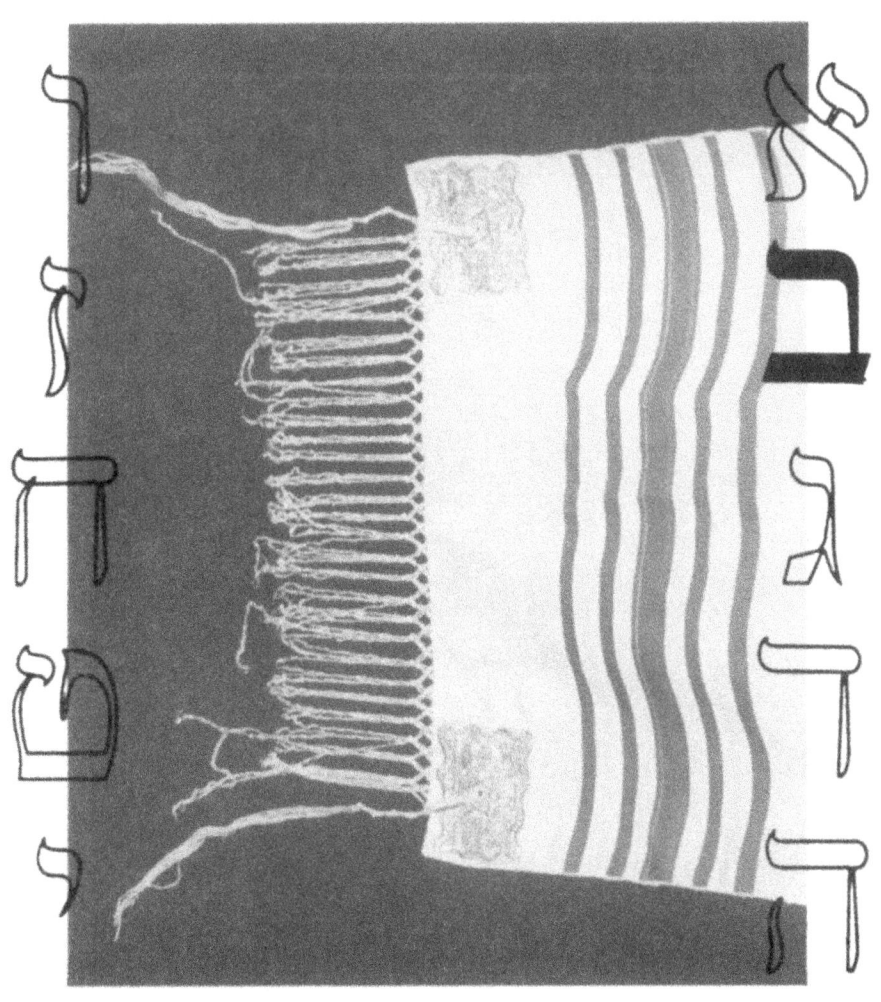

BIRCHOT HASHACHAR
Morning Blessings

There in the dreamworld
the distant spheres
the world whose name
    is formed before our eyes
    by the letters that float there
    when we shade them
    when we shut them
    when we turn our souls
        toward the outside within
    in creation
    in meditation
    in prayer

•

we crouch
close to the ground
absorbing magic from the earth

•

as we slide along the water
across, along, above each other,
our simply being near each other
blending spirits,
like a remote caress

•

as we slide along the water
from the darkness into the light

SHEKHINAH

        as we emerge
        and we brush against the rushes
        as we roll, roll along the banks
        seeing each other,
            the water,
            each other,
            the sky
        the black of the riverbed,
        the black of the night,
        the white of the foam,
        the white of the clouds,
        the blue of the water,
        the blue of the day,
        the black then blue then white
            of expanding circles
            in each other's eyes,
        as if our world were woven from
        the strands of the prayer shawl
        of an unseen mystic

            •

Here in the prayer hall
we speak our words
    just loudly enough
    to be sure that
    we have spoken them correctly,
now pausing for breath,
stand and rock slightly
    to the unmetered rhythms
    of our long-prescribed speech,

            •

MORNING BLESSINGS

speak words of praise to the one
who designed our bodies
   and sculpted our souls
who created the animals,
   earth, and the air

•

for giving us the duty of prayer,
for giving us what freedom we have,
for giving us sight
   and clothes
   and guidance
   and strength

•

for giving us the knowledge
   of good from evil
   of love from hate
   of the world of dreams
      from the world of law

•

        as we slide along the water
          a basket, a raft,
            a small padded platform

•

        on which rests a girlchild
        asleep, silent,
        newly formed
        from the dreams of the creator

•

SHEKHINAH

      a token of his presence
      her hair trailing in the water
      like the light from the tail of a comet
          •

      on her face the gentle smile
      of one who has only known heaven
      her limbs unmoving
      yet speaking in their stillness
      of the potential energy of joy
      waiting for her wakening
          •

      as we slide along the water
      summoned toward the doorway
          in the pillar of smoke
          to which the water flows
      summoned by the voices
          of those who praise
          our common creator
          in ancient words of
              hidden power
      summoned toward the doorway
          to which,
          at the end of days,
          all doors will lead
          •

and we read the prescribed sections
   of the books of the Bible
   of the books of the law
   of the books of the secrets
      of our creation
          •

MORNING BLESSINGS

of how Abraham was called
   to throw away his only son
   (as if Ishmael,
   not yet lost in the wilderness,
   somehow didn't count)
of how Sarah stopped laughing
   when she feared the death of her child,
of how the creator called it off
   when he saw that Abraham would obey,
of how Abraham,
   seeing his child allowed to live
   knew he had found a god
   that he could follow

•

       listening to the voices
          proclaiming the creator
          we slide forward to the door

•

of how Moses was commanded
   how one must prepare
   to approach the altar of sacrifice
of how Aaron was told
   what he must kill,
   and where and when,
of how they prepared the fragrances
   to rise into the air

•

       we approach the pillar
       and in the margins

SHEKHINAH

    between shadow and smoke
   we slide our child onward
     •

of how our teachers fondly described
  in minute detail the Temple laws
of how they prayed
  when the Temple was gone
  and there was no home for sacrifices
of how they replaced
  fire with learning
  slaughter with prayer
  the Temple with the hall of worship
      •

    and bidding farewell
     to the water
     for the moment
    we drift into the doorway
     to the voices
     to the world that waits outside
     far from heaven,
     far from dreams
      •

of how we now determine
  the workings of the law
and yet we pray that we may return
  to the Temple
  to the sacrifices
  to the vivid rituals
  that would speak more clearly

and yet we praise the one
    who placed us where we are today:
        •

Glorified, sanctified is the great name . . .
        •
    Glorified, sanctified is the great name . . .
        •

The voices, in the holiest of prayers,
pull us onward through
the doorway that divides
    the temporary
        from the infinite
    the light of love
        from the light of day
    the distances
          between hand and hand
        from the nearnesses
        of soul to soul
        •

Glorified, sanctified is the great name . . .
        •

into the solid
onto the dry land
into what those who dare not dream
    call the real world
        •

as we pass through the door
our transitions unseen
by those who clothe their souls in earth
        •

SHEKHINAH

    we take on temporary flesh
    and moving
        to their voices
        by the creator's will
          •

we emerge.

Pesukey D'Zimra
פסוקי דזמרה
Verses of Song

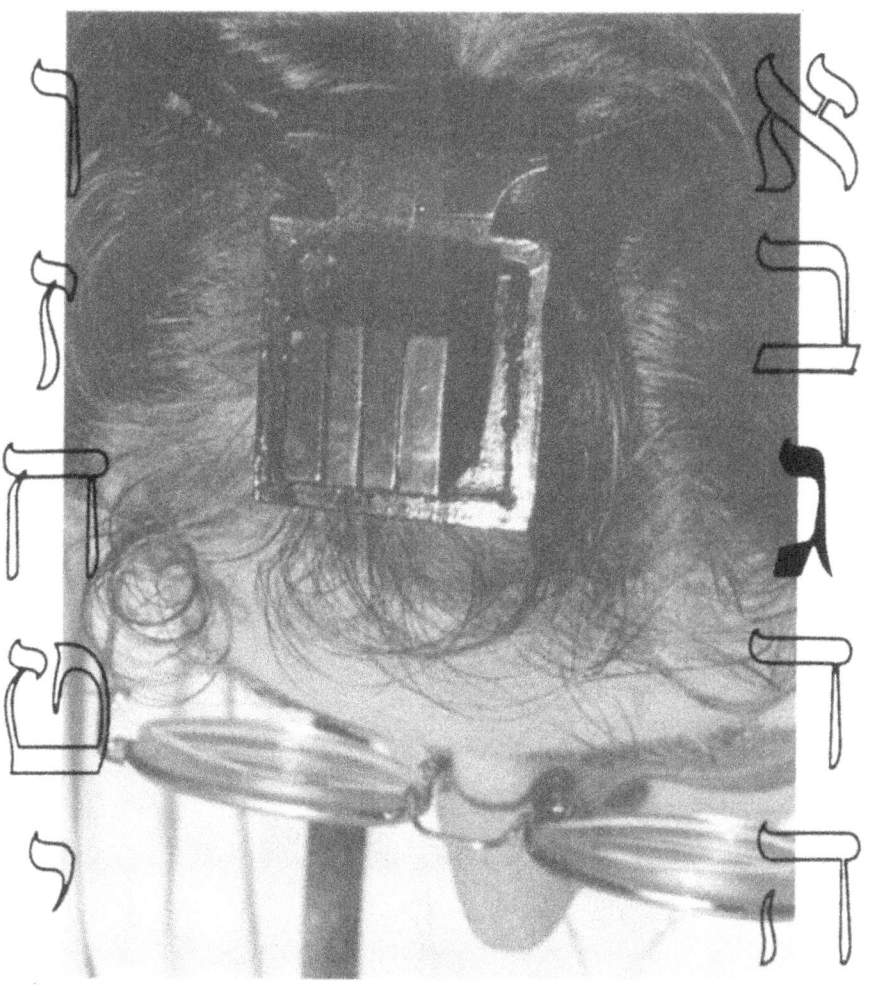

PESUKEY D'ZIMRA
Verses of Song

She is spirit
She is air
She is earth on fire
    above, below the waters

•

She is but a fragment
The least, some say,
    of the shells
    of the Creator

•

but yet
the least part of the infinite
    is greater than
    the greatest of us,
we who are in part defined
    by flesh
    and continuity.

•

She is everywhere
    the creator is;
that is—
she is everywhere

•

SHEKHINAH

yet she is,
most wonderfully,
here

       •

summoned by prayer
summoned by our intent
summoned by our wishes
from the silent world of dreams

       •

Arise, most ancient!
Arise, our mother!
Arise, our bride!
Arise, our daughter!

       •

We raise our eyes
    our hands
    our hearts
    our voice
unto the hills

       •

and sing together
"a song for the dedication of the house"
"a psalm for the thanks-offering"
"a hymn of praise"
and psalm after psalm
"Hallelujah!" (146)
"Hallelujah!" (147)
"Hallelujah!" (148, 149, 150)
and from Chronicles, Chronicles,
    Nehemiah, Exodus

       •

VERSES OF SONG

we praise the Creator
    who may or may not be hearing us
    who may or may not accept us
    who may or may not answer
        our prayers,
        praises,
        supplications
but even those of us who wonder
if the Creator exists at all
    or ever did
    or ever will
join in the song
as if our voices
    can will into existence
    the one whose will
    would have caused us to exist

•

and from the fervent murmur
    of our voices
joined together,
    once per psalm
    in unison,
then breaking apart again
    to the true human rhythm
    where the solitary
    simulates the simultaneous
    like the waves,
        joining, peaking,
        then drifting back
        to independent currents
    like the eagles

SHEKHINAH

      soaring in a seemingly
      common spiral
      (yet, if you watch each one,
      flying a multitude
      of personal air-dances
      of ragged individuality)
            •

arises a more powerful magic
    a common voice
    the syllables we utter
    combining, merging
an incantation of secret names
    that no single voice
    could dare pronounce
an inverse sacred lullaby
          •

and from the slumber
    of the pauses between prayers
    of the passage between planes
    of the journey
        through the spheres
        to this lowest
        (but still needed)
        world
            •

our ancient
    mother
    bride
    child
            •

wakes!

•

and lowering her arms
   opens her eyes
   tests her legs
   (to see whether
     she stands on sky
   or on our far more common
   ground)

•

steps
pauses
steps

•

her legs are the legs
   of a colt
   new to gravity
her arms the wings
   of dragonflies
soft taloned fingers
   those of eagles who
   in unseen gentle moment
   nurture new-hatched young
her body the stem
   of a warm-blooded sunflower
   turning slowly, slowly
   as she

•

SHEKHINAH

pauses
steps
pauses
     •

and focuses our intention
 on her Presence
 on the Presence
  of the Creator
  of this manifestation
   of words of love
   of words of law
     •

(not made flesh, no—
though we can touch her,
 hold her,
 dance with her
 in this extended moment,
still she has no
 failings of the flesh
 and can not ache
 and can not strain
 and can not,
  even for a moment,
  die
yet will be here, real,
while sustained by our intensity,
and little longer
till she must return
 to the world of dreams
 or another hall of prayer)
     •

VERSES OF SONG

and focuses our hearts upon her
      •

and we circle her like planets
 reflecting her light
 upon each other
echoing her movements
      •

and as she moves,
 we move
and as she sings,
 we sing,
and as she wakes the morning world
 we step
 pause
 step
      •

and each in his own manner
every body, every soul,
 adding the motions we have learned
in the pain and joy
 of our existence
repeating and embellishing
 her praisedance
 in private ways
      •

step Hallelujah! (all the earth)
 Hallelujah! (o my soul)
 Hallelujah! (all the angels)
 Hallelujah! (with a new song)
 Hallelujah! (closer, closer)
      •

SHEKHINAH

drawn by joyous gravity
    we circle her,
    we fall in toward her,
    longing for her
    to embrace the Presence
        grasp the heart of prayer
        lay our hands upon the holy
          •

and our leader calls out,
"Glorified!
Sanctified!
is the Great Name!"
          •

and we move to melt into the Presence,
    lose ourselves in her,
    she who loves and comforts,
    she whose power is such
    that we forget ourselves and
        •

move
to
lose
our
selves
        •

in
      •

joy!

BORCHU

ברכו

Bless the Lord

BORCHU
Bless the Lord

Bless the Lord, who is blessed!
   •

Our leader returns,
her arms waving
semaphores and signals,
disrupting our focus,
returning our eyes
    voices
    hearts
to the service we are sworn to perform
returning our attention
    to the call to the Creator
        who demands prayer
           attention
           obedience
        away from the Presence,
           his Presence in her form
               she who radiates love
                  comfort
                  joy
              •

We breathe and turn,
    delaying,
    denying ourselves

SHEKHINAH

    the ecstasy
    for the moment
until we can complete
    the patterns of prayer
    dictated by law
    and debated by teachers
    over the centuries,
    yet still, in their variations,
    very close to the same;
               •

any one of us,
transported to a hall of prayer
anywhere in our world
would recognize the litany
and find comfort in its cadences,
              •

another door which is all doors,
another portal of words
    which connects our world
        to a world without words
    our world today
        to the world to come,
        or, at least,
        to the world to which
        each of us,
        individually,
        may someday come
            •

though we know well
(some more consciously than others)
that the world to come

BLESS THE LORD

    is already here,
that we may dwell within it
    and it within us
    in our prayers
        meditations
        fantasies
        dreams
that the stillness of the Sabbath
    is a precreation
    of what we will
    (someday, somehow)
    see.

•

"Bless the Lord, who is blessed!"

•

calls our leader,
and the phrase loops back on itself
in its simplicity

•

the Lord is blessed,
    so we must bless the Lord
the Lord is blessed,
    and from the Lord derives all blessing
    so how could we bless the Lord?
the Lord is blessed
    and blesses all of us

•

so we bless the Lord
as the Lord has blessed us,
our blessings
    the reflections in a pitted mirror

SHEKHINAH

    of the blessings he bestows on us
our souls
    reaching out, reaching in
    trying to find and echo
    the shards of the infinite
    embedded, glowing deep within us,
our hearts
    pulsing with a rhythm
        (in the silence of true meditation
        we can hear it, feel it)
    that we hope may match the
    breaths and tempos
    of the root tone of the universe
our voices
    when we raise them in song
        all in tune
        all in key
        all in rhythm
    so that when we find and share
        the central tone
        the pulse beat
            of the heart of the Lord
        the frequency, the pitch and color
        of the Lord's power,
        the Lord's Presence
            (who stands among us
            surrounded by us,
            surrounding us
            joining us,
            her glowing resonance
            synchronized with

BLESS THE LORD

              the power of the Lord
              her ancient
                  father
                  groom
                  child)
the shards in our souls
may again
    emerge
    merge
    vibrate
    fuse
    and join all worlds
        with the greater world
                ●

so we bless the Lord
calling back to our leader
                ●

"Blessed is the Lord who is blessed
    now and in eternity"
    here and out to other worlds
blessed
    praised
        glorified
            exalted
                upraised
every soul will the bless the Lord
    who is blessed
    who is blessing
                ●

those of us who may or may not be
    blessing the Lord

SHEKHINAH

who may or may not be
    caught up in the
    circle of blessing
still feel the prayer that flows
    from (to)
    the hearts of the believers
        •

those of us who may or may not
    believe
still share the words
    so that from the words
    from the letters and silences
    of the prayers we might
    deconstruct and reconstruct
        rebuild
        rephrase
        reinterpret
    these feelings
    into new prayers
        new statements
        new beliefs
    that might resonate
        with our own hearts
            minds
            souls
    and with the different tone
        of the prayer
            as written
            as spoken
            as believed
        •

BLESS THE LORD

by those of us
who do fervently believe

•

Blessed is the Lord who is Blessed
    forever and ever

        •

as our leader proclaims
    repeating our response as her own

        •

then
withdrawing
from this moment
of joined voices
and statements
simple in words
yet tangled in meaning

        •

we pray the details
all of our voices
    joined yet unjoined
speaking larger yet smaller words
    in private utterances
together, yet unsynchronized

        •

and the Presence
    for that moment focused
    in a single beam of holiness
diffuses
    spreads
    surrounds us

        •

SHEKHINAH

and we grasp the Presence
    our hands warmed
    by the contact
    the warmth spreading
    through us from the touch
        as the night chill
            dissipates
        as the sun appears to rise
            from the East, behind the Ark
        as the beams and shadows
            shorten, widen,
        as we spin toward it,
            until it, later,
                meets and illuminates
                    the roof of the sky
                      •

and we raise her up
and she raises us up
and she spreads her arms
    (slender,
        like the legs of grasshoppers,
    gentle,
        like the wings of swans,
    lithe,
        like the upraised branches
        of an inverted willow)
and echoes our leader's
    signs and cries of supplication
                •

as our legs,
supporting us,

BLESS THE LORD

and, by extension,
supporting her
    as her radiance,
    in its fields of power
    supports our souls
echo the steps of our leader
through the pathways of the law
    the litanies we speak together
    the unseen trails
        of the wonders of which we speak

          •

as we move and speak
    in the phrases of our Teachers
    in the motions of our leader
    in the comfort of the Presence
    of the actions of the Lord
        echoing
        cascading
        rippling out
        like the wake of a skipped stone
            upon the surface of
            what was once
            unformed and uniform
            undistilled and undifferentiated
            until a word
            Let there be
        spread among
            the sacred and the mundane
        and formed the frames of radiance

          •

SHEKHINAH

that
illuminate the Earth
    and those who dwell upon it . . .
created glory for his Name,
    and placed luminaries
    about his majesty . . .
the leaders of his legions,
    the holy ones . . .
    the ministering angels,
    who stand at
        the summit of the universe . . .
beloved,
flawless,
mighty

        •

and our leader,
hearing our independent streams of prayer
    approach the merging point,
    the delta where prayer
    comes again together,
calls out:

        •

"and they all give each other permission
to sanctify the One who created them
    in tranquility
    with pure speech
    and sacred melody
and all proclaim in reverence
    in holiness:"

        •

and our voices merge
and our songs and bodies move together,
    we,
    our leader,
    the Presence
        (with her ever-widening glow),
    those who believe,
    those who may or may not believe,
    the Seraphim,
    the Ofanim,
    all the holy beings,
    one joined people
    and ten levels of angels,
    proclaiming:

        •

"*Holy!*" (we rise up on pointed toes)
"*Holy!*" (rise higher,
    straining toward the heavens)
"*Holy!*" (that the glow of the Presence
    might meet
    the light of the Creator)
"*is the Lord, Master of Legions!*
The world is filled with his Glory!"

        •

and we overflow,
    run,
    dance,
to the sweet melodies of the creation
    to which our souls sing harmony
    in as many keys
    as there are people,

SHEKHINAH

    souls,
    and angels

•

and we try to merge our souls
    as we might gather together the fringes
        from the four corners of
          our prayer shawls
    as we might be gathered to the Presence
        from the four corners of
          the Earth
    as we might be gathered into
the World to Come
        from all the corners
        the nooks and lost alleyways
        of present, imagined, and parallel
            lines of time

•

and we close our eyes
as our leader stops her motion,
and, in a sudden moment of infinite silence,
locks her eyes with the eyes of the Presence
and we, focusing with light-fused wills
    the intensity of our intention,
    prepare to proclaim
    the core of our existence in a
    unified joyful cry.

Shema
שמע
Listen

SHEMA
Listen

Six words.

              •

We say them clearly
   distinctly
our hands closing our eyes
as we enunciate
   each letter
   each unwritten vowel
   each silence between words
              •

One wrong letter
   and the meaning is blasphemy
One wrong vowel
   and the meaning is in doubt
One misplaced silence
   and the meaning is at best obscured.
             •

Six words.
              •

We focus on the One Creator,
the Unity,
forgetting for the moment
   all manifestations
   all simple evidence

SHEKHINAH

    even the solidity of
        his Presence.

                •

She, alone,
floats above us,
    weightless,
    glowing,
    rejoicing,
joining in our proclamation.

                •

Her love and power pour down on us
like the gentle rain
    that does not disrupt
    the white-globed dandelions
and she turns
facing in all directions
yet at all times facing east.

                •

She, too, chants clearly,
showing no envy
toward the One of whom she is
    a partner and a part
    a mate and an emanation
showing her closeness
    to us and to the One
    at a careful distance
so that we may concentrate fully
on the One without distraction.

                •

She floats,
her love and focus

LISTEN

joining with ours
as we chant

•

Six words

•

in the ancient sacred language
(though like so many words
they expand and lose some focus
when moved away into other tongues):

•

Hear
    We chant aloud
    as our words sail forth
    beyond the solid chambers of
    this sacred hall.

•

We chant aloud
these ancient words
going back
    to the ages of the Holy Books
    to the days of Moses
    to the nights of Solomon

•

back to these words
    which rose from the lips of believers
        from the lips of martyrs

•

always making sure
that they were heard
    by other believers
        and potential believers

SHEKHINAH

    by our tormentors
        as a sign
        that their iron combs
        could not flay our spirits
    by the One
        as a proclamation,
        and, for some,
        as a prayer that the One
        might believe equally in us.
                •

Israel
  and most importantly,
  that we heard ourselves and each other
  proclaiming unity
      of the One
      in the One
      for the One
  proclaiming ourselves
      to be of the ones
      who chose,
          or were chosen by,
          or chose to be chosen by,
      the One we follow.
              •

"We will do them;
we will hear them"
our ancestors said of the
    forthcoming laws
conveying trust
(or perhaps extreme self-confidence)

LISTEN

that whatever the One would command us
we would promise to fulfill.
      •

"We will do them;
we will hear them"
in that order.
The stars arranged themselves
  above Mount Sinai
  as a dotted line
and, with an invisible quill
  made of the feathers
  of all the doves
  who would give their souls
    in sacrifice
with weightless ink
  comet's-tail white
  made of the blood
    of sacrifice and martyrdom
  blended with the tears
    of Sarah,
      believing Isaac was no more,
    of Hannah,
      who prayed that, like Sarah,
      she might someday see a son,
    of all the mothers
      who died, and saw others die,
      in pogroms,
        wars, and
        holocausts,
with a giant hand
  formed of the will of generations

SHEKHINAH

    its lifeline stretching
        from the past to the unknown
    its fingers spread
        in the secret sacred salute
        to which, when our priests
        repeated it in blessing,
        the Presence would come,
        for a moment, to rest
    its pulsing veins
        arrayed in the emulation
        of the brief holy name
        that the leather strands
        around our merely human hands
        now follow

•

we signed the eternal covenant
and met the strong hand
    and outstretched arm
    of the One
and shook on it
reaffirming the contract
    made with Noah
        and bonded by the rainbow
    made with Abraham
        in the field of visions
        where the flaming torch
            and smoking oven
        moved among
        the half-animals they sacrificed
    made with Jacob
        at Bethel

LISTEN

>   before his favorite son
>   was born
>   before his wife and his father
>   died
>   before
>   (emboldened by the knowledge
>   that he would share
>   in his fathers' inheritance)
>   he joined for one last
>   peaceful moment
>   with his spurned angry brother
>   to bury their father,
>   embracing Esau at Hebron
>   before their sons resumed
>   their interminable wars.

•

"We will do them;
we will hear them"
and with these words
our ancestors changed
from a random band of refugees
    into a people
still to have to wait to find a land
still to have to pass through cycles
    of conquest
        exile
        wandering, and
        return
still (their name showing that
    their ancestor had wrestled
    with messengers of the One)

SHEKHINAH

    wrestling with their own beliefs
    trying to find adaptations
        interpretations
        re-creations
    to make the ancient words fit
    the changing worlds
    in which we must survive.
            •

The Lord
    Despite the insistence
        on clarity
            accuracy
            consistency
            •

we do not
spell this word as spoken,
speak this word outside of prayer
    (with even the substitutions
    we speak now)
write this word in such a way
    that we might deduce
    from simple letters and from vowels
    how we would pronounce it
    if we were to dare
        disobey the warnings
        of teachers and mystics
        that from these four letters
        miracles are made.
            •

Even the way we pronounce it
within prayer

within readings of the holy books
is a mystery.
The Name of the One
seems to be plural,
not, as we translate the Name,
"Lord"
but rather,
"Lords"
as if showing that within
    One is All,
as if saying that
    the One that commands
    the One that blesses
    the One that gives
        and takes away
    all are the One

•

and, as we pronounce it,
the Name is personal,
not, a simple distant object,
"The Lord,"
but rather,
"My Lords"
as if showing the connection
    in a single word
as if saying that
    the One that creates
    the One that watches
    the One that rewards

SHEKHINAH

      and disciplines
    all speak to us
               •

is our God
    and now, another name,
    this one softer,
    pronounced as spelled
              •

    whereas, they say,
    the first name denotes judgement,
    this name denotes mercy
              •

    and the holy books
    use first one name,
    then another,
    showing, some say,
        aspects of the One
        visible in that part of the story
    showing, according to others,
        who wrote that part of the story
        and when
        and, perhaps, why
            •

    and this name, too,
    is strangely plural,
    as is the hidden verb
        nestled between the names
            •

    "My Lords are our Gods"?
            •

LISTEN

    the struggle
        between meaning and vocabulary
        between statement, sense, and syntax
        between the words on our lips
            and the feelings in our hearts
        •
    compels us to drive onward
        •

The Lord
        again,
        again stating the first name,
        the ineffable name,
        spoken from the depths of sacred mystery
        with the sounds of an unrelated word
        spelled, through our teachers'
            well-intentioned indirection
        with the vowels of the spoken word,
        leading those who dared to speak them
            devoid of special powers,
                the ashes of the burnt husk
                    of what seemed to be the name
                dry and bitter
                on their erring tongues
        •
    and even these mistakes
    were judged unsafe by our teachers
    who told us not to speak the holy name
    nor even to utter the second name,
        the mask that hid the Tetragrammaton,
        except in carefully controlled
            environments

SHEKHINAH

    except when at the height of prayer
instead we only say "The Name"
    as if, by saying the name of the Name,
    we name that
        to which we mean to refer,
    the One who rests
    under layers of onion skin
    inscribed by those
        schooled in the sacred,
    removed from being one with the Earth
        by the layers of metaphor
            in which he is clothed
        by the emanations and manifestations
            which mediate and interfere
    making sure that only the purest souls,
        the most stubborn,
    pierce through the symbols
    and come to rest
    in the highest of heavens
    next to the throne of the One
    while we down here are comforted
        by his partner self,
        his Presence,
    sheltering us as we speak the words
    (the strangely plural,
        the misleadingly pronounced,
        the ineffable)
    that proclaim the Unity,
        the identity,
        of the name we dare not speak

•

LISTEN

is One
            of the One.
                    •

At last it rests on this:
that in all the confusion
    of names and numberings,
    of inscription and pronunciation
    of the repetitive
        the hidden and
        the oddly plural
the One,
    who is named by every sound
    whose image resonates with
        the paths of planets and stars
    whose scent is carried
        by every breeze that
        drifts through memories,
        masking, for the moment,
        the mundane truth
        transmitted by the air,
is One.
                    •

And our teachers have told us
to say this twice each day
with the intent to make it seem
that this simplest of statements
the core of all we speak in prayer
is a new revelation
    never before heard
    never before exposed

SHEKHINAH

      now brought again to light
    for us to contemplate.
                •

and we pause,
                •

then whisper the prayer that Moses
    was said to have learned
    from the angels:
                •

"Blessed is the name
* of the glory of his kingdom*
* forever."*
                •

(again we say that the Blessed is blessed
again we speak of the name, not the One,
and of his kingdom which is everywhere
    the Creator is;
that is—
everywhere)
                •

then speak of the places and times
where we have been commanded
    to remember the six holy words
and the source of the shawl
    and the boxes and the straps
      with which we wrap and bind ourselves.
                •

And the Presence spins and lowers,
weaving a bright sheer web of holiness
about our leader
                •

LISTEN

then, gently,
she brings us together

·

after our grand statements
    our bold proclamations
there will soon be silence

·

with her tiny, powerful hands
with her seemingly fragile fingertips
that carved the words of the One
    with letters of fire
    into slabs of stone

·

she transfers a kiss of silence
    to our minds
        our lips
        our hearts
        our hands

·

and we all stand together
we each stand alone
all as one in her eyes
all made equal by her touch
each locked
    in a silent secret focus
    by the power of her kiss

·

as we stand and face the east
and her beauty blends with the rays
of the now risen sun

·

SHEKHINAH

as we prepare ourselves for these meditations
•
together
alone
•
in silence.

AMIDAH
עמידה
Silent Prayer

AMIDAH
Silent Prayer

Silence

no

words spoken

here

we

now

stand

tightly joined
together

alone

three steps back
three steps forward
as we approach the ghost of a throne

feet held closely together

SHEKHINAH

"Oh Lord, open our lips . . ."
                    •

For each blessing
meticulously written
we bend our knees and bow
then stand erect again
and turn and sway
              •

and as we speak the prayers
in silence
we listen also
to the whisperings of our hearts.
              •

Listen: you may hear
    the turning of pages
    the hum of the lights
    the rush of traffic passing outside
    the rustle of moving lips
        as we mouth and savor
        the ancient texts
    the shuffle of feet.
              •

Listen: if you hear these,
    listen more closely.
             •

(The Presence comes near,
    tentatively,
    as if afraid that her light
    will distract us from
    our focus.
             •

SILENT PRAYER

She moves among us
    silent
    unseen

        •

Then, with further joy,
    exchanging power with us
    as the beams of our prayers merge and
        point east
        point upward
        point outward

        •

She runs in paths of symbols of infinity
    bowing and swirling among us
    her energies reflecting,
    refracting our movements
    our bows and turns
    tilting, spinning her outward

        •

until
as each of us completes the prayer
    (three steps forward
    three steps back)
she slows

        •

then once again rejoins the silence
    standing,
    waiting to the east)

        •

We finish

        •

SHEKHINAH

and our leader turns,
then turns back,

          •

reprising
saying the prayers again, aloud,
    for those who may not have prayed
    for those who may not have understood
    for those who may not have listened
        to their inner selves
        to their voices of meditation.
          •

We stand
          •

and,
more relaxed,
more aligned with the surrounding atmosphere
          •

let our minds drift
to the leader's melodies
as we
and the shielding hall of prayer
become one.

Kriyat Hatorah
קריאת התורה
Reading

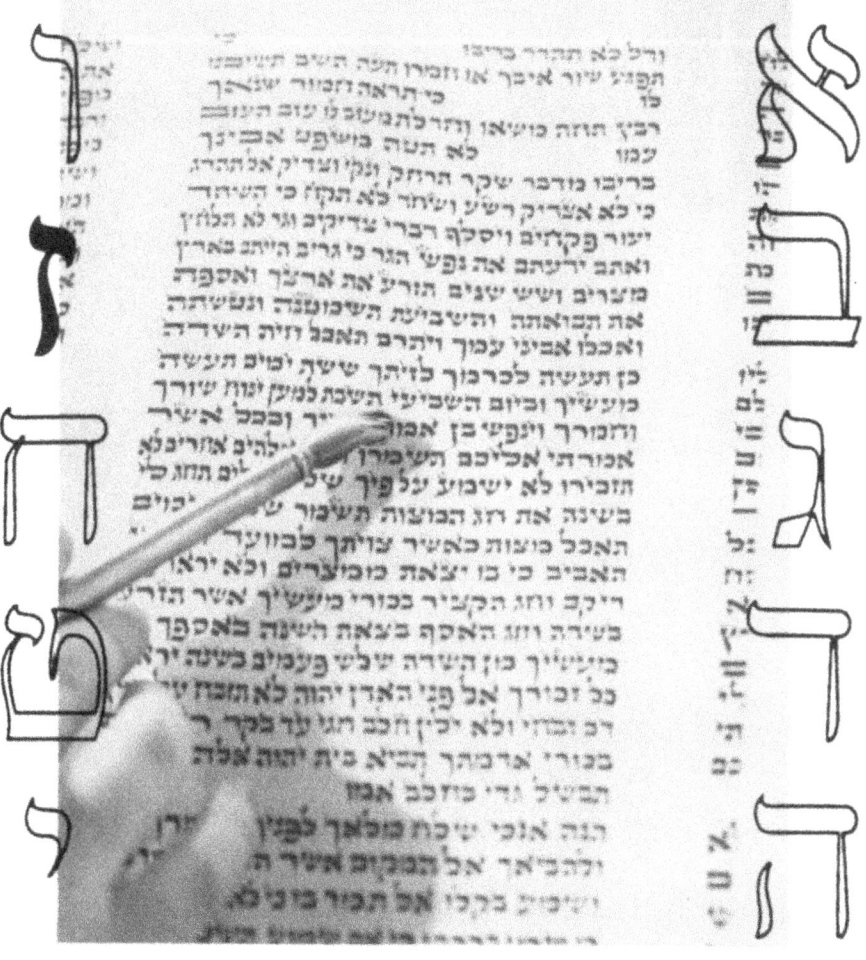

KRIYAT HATORAH
Reading

These ancient walls
These silent speaking stones
These wooden seatbacks
    worn smooth
    by the books and hands
    of generations
               •

In the haze of words and tones
of our leader's repetition
we float our souls
in search of others
similarly focused
                •

to Brooklyn
to Vilna
to Yemen
to Jerusalem
                •

to the chambers by the Western Wall
to the place that,
    when all places become one,
    will be the one place
    those places will become
               •

SHEKHINAH

to the place where the dreamworld
    the world to come
    the world from which
        we were called here
        summoned to take on
        temporary flesh
    brushes closest to
this world in which we breathe.

•

Step up to the Western Wall,
facing east
(we pray at what was
    the outside of the temple,
    the inside having drawn the faithful
        of other faiths
        of other tastes of God
    to establish their own
        solemn sacred domains within),
kiss the stones,
slide a bit of paper in
    within the cracks
    between the massive bricks
    where so many others
        have inserted their own prayers
    in hopes that God will read
        these small requests
        with greater interest,
step back one step,
turn left, and face

•

READING

another wall
of arches,
    doorways,
    gates,
    and somewhat less ancient stone.

•

Walk through the nearer arch.

•

Here: a small chamber
    dressed in stone on stone.
    Wooden bookshelves line its walls,
    filled with well-worn volumes:
        books of prayer,
        books of law,
            psalms,
            mysteries, and
            commentaries.

•

Lift one book down.
Open it: the pages are yellow, brittle,
    brought from a town that no longer lives
        a town whose ashes
        and the ashes of its citizens
        still drift in the air over
            Poland, Hungary, Austria
        still sting the eyes,
        still trigger sudden tears
            for those (now older, now scattered)
            who survived the war

•

SHEKHINAH

    (and few recall the gentle storms
        whose raindrops caught the ashes
           souls
           letters
        and carried them back to earth
        grounding the microscopic angels
           who were guiding them to Jerusalem.
               •

    Listen: in the dim silence
        of dawn-lit desert roads
        you can hear them
        walking back eastward
               •

        to ascend again to heaven
        from the welcoming shadow
        of the Temple Mount.)
               •

Walk on, walk forward
a few steps more, another archway
then a cavelike hall extending to the left
from which echo remnants
    of the voices of students
    present, past, and yet to come
    who sit within cavern-rooms
        by the light of candles
        by the light of the sun
    and argue fine points
        of the laws and mysteries
        again and again.
               •

READING

(The walls have heard
these arguments so frequently
that the stones themselves have memorized
the cases, counterpoints, and deductions.
•

Look closely: the veins of rhetoric and logic
    are embedded deep within
      the porous rock.)
•

Do not turn there;
walk forward, walk on.
To your right: grate-covered shafts
    expose more of the Western Wall
    down to where the ground had been
    when Solomon built it there.
To your left: another bookcase
    more volumes
    some different
    but mostly the same
    and small signs urging that you treat
      the books and rooms
        with due proper respect for
        their sanctity and antiquity.
•

Ahead again, again to the left:
another arch, another gate.
Iron bars run floor to ceiling,
    to the smoothly curved arch
    set in time-cooled stone.
The gates are open,

SHEKHINAH

    swung back into corners,
    welcoming us within.
                      •

We have arrived.
                      •

Before us: The Arks
    up a series of steps
    stand
    dressed in fine, polished wood
    wearing curtains of velvet
        of golden braid
        with golden threaded
        letters and images
            lions
            tablets
            quotations
                      •

Touch the curtains gently:
the softness of the velvet
    caresses our fingers
the roughness of the golden script
    transfers its meaning
    from hands to souls and hearts,
    in holy braille.
Our eyes, our minds can only see
    the edges of the glory;
we open wide our senses
    and absorb the moment
        the distant sounds
        the promise of the Presence
    through breath

through touch
through the resonance of centuries
   of wanderers and pilgrims
    whose prayers,
      dreams,
      ecstasies
    have accumulated here;
    the echoes of their souls
    still coat the grey stone walls
    long after their bodies
      no longer walk these roads.

•

And these Arks,
   these cases and curtains,
are echoes of the first holy Ark
   that was built in the desert
   that contained the twin tablets
    of the essence of the law
   that traveled to Israel
   that went into battle
   that came to rest upstairs from here
    in the original Temple
    in the holiest of places
   that was the resting place of the Presence
    when she came to stay with us
   that disappeared into history
    buried, some say, in a hidden mountain
      to be retrieved
      when the Temple is rebuilt
      in the world to come
    carried, some say, to the world of dreams

SHEKHINAH

      where we will gather
      where time is silent
      where the rivers carry angels
          to and from our world of flesh.
         •

Look now;
Feel;
Lay your hands upon the curtains;
Grasp and follow the opening cords:
         •

In this moment, all Arks are one.
We concentrate on the moment
   with a focus greater than reality.
We look beyond the present
   beyond these chambers in Jerusalem
   beyond the prayer hall
      where we still also stand.
All images merge:
the curtains form a single canopy of velvet
   its folds waving in and out
   of the three mundane dimensions
   its length, its texture, its embrace
      wider, deeper than the sky
a single glowing golden thread
   creating, joining all the letters
      symbols
      images
   into a single pictogram
      which, if we could but pronounce it,

would join all of the holy Names
into a single syllable of joy
•

and at its center
   (that is—
   everywhere)
the image of the original Ark
•

On its curtain, infinitely tall,
   portrayed in gold,
   their bodies closer to ideal
   than any human artist's
   craft, conception, calculation,
•

Cherubim—angels, intermediaries—
stand and wait
infinitely patient
listening to heaven
formed from the souls of clouds
(Male and female he created them)
•

They need not speak;
the Ofanim, the Seraphim
call out, at times,
bless the Blessed
from his holy place.
•

From this holy place,
the Cherubim need not call;
the Presence is forever here
•

SHEKHINAH

    and thus they stand
    side by side
    their contact sign enough
        of their love of the Presence
        of their love of each other
        of their love of humankind.
            •

Approach the Ark, then,
(in the hall of prayer,
    in Jerusalem,
    in the near and distant
        world of dreams)
touch the shoulder of a cherub
    the cord of a curtain
    the place within your heart
        which leads you to
        what rests inside the Ark,
open the gates,
    the everlasting doors,
    that we may see the mysteries
    that lie concealed within,
and the doors, the curtains,
    at the breath of a touch
    from our solemn, exultant leader,
part and open wide for us
    like frost on a mirror
        at the warming exhalation
        of one who is still alive
    like the waters of the Sea of Reeds
        before Moses's unyielding staff
    like the thighs of a long-accustomed lover

READING

      at a gentle touch
      a familiar embrace

•

And we gaze within and see

•

The Scroll of the Law,
    covered, also, in velvet
    lettered, also, in threads of gold
    the fine-lathed spools,
        her arms and legs,
        crafted from the richest wood
    her cool skin
        formed from the purest of parchment
    the meticulous letters,
        black pools of eyes
        glistening upon the
            pale white background
        reading us as we read from her
    a slender silver arm reaching downward
        guiding us to see the words
        from which we draw our life.

•

Carefully, now, our leader
embraces
then raises the scroll,
bringing her out
    from the eternal womb of the Ark
    into the merely physical
    light of the now-risen sun

•

SHEKHINAH

(The Cherubim part,
    then move silently around our leader
    and crouch before us,
    silent guardians of the Holy Word)
        •

and gently, slowly, evenly,
with the strength and balance gained
by uncounted years
of practice and devotion,
        •

lifts
        •

the scroll into the air,
shining her pearl-sheen light upon us
    as we rise to greet
    the unveiling of her Words
    with scattered unison
    whisperings of our own,
raising her closer to the skies
    as she brings the breath of heaven
        closer to our lives
    and inspires the spark of the Eternal
        buried deep within us
        to burn more strongly
        to melt another fraction
            of the husks of darkness
            that surround and mask the sparks
            that make our world remain distant
                from the world of dreams
        •

READING

then, again slowly, again gently,
brings her back down
back to the grasp
   of those of us who honor her
back down to our realm to accept our kiss
      •

but we dare not kiss her directly, no,
lest she be defiled by the lips of those of us
   who have allowed words of evil,
      of human hurt,
         distrust, and battered truth
   to be formed by them
   to pass between them
lest her holy glow of love burn our mouths
   making us as slow of speech as Moses
   with no inspired, willing Aaron
   to speak for us the words we try to mean
      •

and so we clutch the corners of
our prayer shawls in our trembling hands
and, as she passes,
kiss the cloth, and the fringes on it,
then touch it softly to her velvet cloak.
      •

And, having travelled, having blessed
the perimeters of our sacred hall,
she rests
relaxed on her back on the reading desk,
   its surface covered, also, in velvet,
   its fringes, also, threads of gold.
Carefully we remove her silver ornaments:

SHEKHINAH

    her crown, circled with subtle filigree,
        rests on a platform by the Ark;
    her pointer, her hand,
        olive wood with silver chain,
        the leader holds,
        preparing for the reading.
              •

Cautiously we raise her again
from her resting place,
and remove her cloak,
    slowly, smoothly.
Upwards our hands slide it,
    along the smooth firmness
        of her parchment torso
        over the slender symmetry
           of her dark wood spools and arms.
            •

We lay her down again,
and roll the columns outwards,
exposing her night-black text
    and pale white skin
    to the eastern light
        of the glass-refracted sun
    to the cooling breezes
        of dim Jerusalem halls
    to our loving gaze
        and shyly tender touch
as the leader extends a well-trained hand
    that holds the simple pointer
    and its own silver hand.
            •

READING

We shall begin.

•

*"And may his kingship over us be revealed
and become visible soon
and may he be gracious to our remnant
    and the remnant of his people
    the family of Israel
for graciousness, kindness, mercy, and favor"*

•

And we respond,
"Amen."

•

Listen, now;
awake from your reveries;
the leader is calling you,

•

*"Descendant of priests,
approach, arise"*

•

speaking a name
that you realize must be your own,
and another name,
which must be your father.

•

Step up to the reading desk,
slowly, slowly;
in these moments of revelation
you have infinite time.

•

(The dreamworld is fading for you now;
this temporary flesh

SHEKHINAH

in which you clothed yourself
when called from the river
    where you guided the child's ark
        toward the Ark of the covenant
    where you drifted homeward
        summoned by voices of prayer
feels slightly more concrete now,
    more confining:

•

you have been called by your name
    and the name of your father.
A lineage has been thrust upon you:
The weight of centuries
    now rests on your shoulders;
the decisions of the fathers
    delimit the children
    far past the tenth generation.

•

Descendant of priests,
the law has determined
    that you are first in line
        to be called to read from the holy scrolls
    that you may bless the people,
        your hands spread in the unseen salute
            that so many know
            and so few recognize
                the Presence resting gently
                on your outstretched fingers
    that you and your fathers and sons
        will be called
            in the world to come

READING

      in the world beyond dreams
      to celebrate the sacrifices
         and forgotten rituals
      in the third temple
         the everlasting hall
         the sanctuary, outside of time,
            from which the plans
               for lesser sanctuaries were drawn.

•

Thus, by your name encircled,
    enabled,
    drawn,
    defined

•

you take a deeper breath
    of this world's air
and move infinitely slowly
    to the reading desk
    to her resting place,
        she who defines all worlds.)

•

"Bless the Lord, who is blessed!"

•

Again, your words wrap back upon themselves,
    reiterating, restating,
    repeating the recursion

•

"now and in eternity!"

•

SHEKHINAH

We carry the phrases as before
    in a feedback loop of blessing
                •

"who has chosen us from all peoples
    and has given us your teaching"
                •

Focus your heart on the text, now,
    on the beauty and glory
    unrolled before you.
The leader points to the appointed words;
grasp the prayer shawl fringes
    in your silent hand
then touch them
    to the black, enveloping letters
then kiss them
                •

and listen
and merge your inner voice
    with the voice of the leader
    with the words that rise
        from the holy scroll
        from her pale, near-glowing skin,
        from her heart.
                •

Clearly, emphatically,
the reader sings out the words of the text,
each vowel, each note, all punctuation
    ringing out from memory
    unwritten in the text as seen
    but deeply etched in tradition.
                •

READING

The pointer hand,
   olive wood and silver,
   a perfected echo of the human hand
      that guides it
      smoothly, lightly,
      along the letters
      (black as the pupils
         of the eyes of the soul)
traces the text,
revealing the words
   that flow up through it
   absorbed and transmitted
   by the skin
      the nerves
      the sinews
      the blood
      the breath
      the heart
      the voice of the reader
   through the air
      through the ether
      through the light
         that underlies all space
         that overlays all time
   to all our hearts.

•

And these words
   that we hear now
   fill the room
   fill every hidden crevice of silence

SHEKHINAH

    that might have been left behind
    by the now-departed night.
        •

(Listen: in the light of the fully risen sun
    even the crickets have muted their song
    in honor of the chant of our leader
      of the repetition, the recitation
      of the words of the law.)
        •

And when the selection has come to an end
    when our leader has finished
      the impassioned reading
    when the melodies of meaning
      find their final major cadence
        •

reach down again,
    fingers still wrapped
      in the tassels of the shawl
touch the tender scroll again,
then kiss, again, the tassels.
        •

"You are blessed,"
you call out to the Creator
*"who gave us these teachings of truth
and planted eternal life in our midst."*
        •

And you step back, away,
around to the side of the reading desk
        •

READING

and another approaches,
and another still,
    •

and the scroll waits for their approach,
her columns lying open to their touch,
    their kiss,
    their prayers
    •

and she gives of her words,
    her light, her love,
    equally to all
    who come to her with open hearts,
    who call to her with willing souls.
    •

Then, all readings complete for the day,
    (though the reading, the learning
        is never complete,
    and the words cycle endlessly
        as the dawn whispers across the planet,
        as the years draw us around the sun,
    as, on this day in other ages,
        our fathers, our children,
        have read, will read,
        the same pages, the same texts,
        from physically different scrolls,
        letter for letter, point for point,
            the same
        as the original letters, inscribed at Sinai,
            in black fire on white fire
            on pages of stone,
            burning through the ages,

SHEKHINAH

      all scrolls joined end to end
          across dimensions,
     flowing, black pools of letters
         endlessly deep,
         sacred scrolls all joined at the text)
our leader softly grasps the scroll's dark wood limbs
rolls her columns close, again, together,
and raises her, again, high into the air.

             •

"She is a tree of life for those who hold her,"
we chant, *"and those who support her*
   are filled with joy.
All her ways are pleasant;
all her paths are peace."

             •

"And may it be the will," our leader replies,
"of our Father who is in heaven
to establish the Temple, the home of our lives,
and to restore his Presence among us,
speedily,
in our time."

             •

Then we all join the leader,
and together,
quietly,
chant
"Amen."

             •

And our leader
lowers her, evenly
   with the perfect balance

READING

    born of perfect faith
and cradles her,
    head resting
       in comfort, in love,
       against her solid side,
    nestling the other side
       in the crook of an arm,
    right hand lightly grasping
       her finely lathed spindle leg,

•

and circles, again, the congregation,
and again we kiss the scroll by proxy
    hand wrapped in tassels,
    tassels touched to lips,
    kiss transferred by tassels' touch
       to our beloved,
       to our law

•

And you sit upon the simple chair
provided on the podium
and the leader rests the scroll
    in your waiting arms,
    her back resting against your chest
       (breathe lightly, now,
       so that you won't disturb her),
    her slender legs straddling your thigh,
    her weight against you,
       heavier than flesh
       but still warm with comfort.

•

SHEKHINAH

"May it be the will
  of our Father who is in heaven,"
The congregation meditates
on ancient words again,
their silence again the scattered unison
  of the individual,
  the universal,
as the leader continues the litany of wishes:
"to have mercy on us,
  on those of us who still remain to worship . . .
to keep destruction and plague
  from us and from all his people . . .
to preserve among us our sages,
  their mates,
  their children,
  their disciples and
    the students of their disciples . . .
that we may be told of good tidings
  of deliverance and comfort . . .
that he gather the dispersed
  from the four corners of the earth . . .
that he may have mercy on our brethren
  who are handed over to distress and captivity,
  on the sea or on dry land,
  and may bring them
    from darkness to light,
    from servitude to liberty,
    speedily, soon . . ."
                               •

  Focus, again:
    The Ark again is open,

READING

    the Cherubim by its edges, waiting,
    the velvet throne room
        coffin
        womb
    awaiting her return.

            •

Sense, feel, open your eyes:
    she must return soon to her home.
    Cautiously the leader
        lifts her forward,
        tightens, again, her columns together,
        ties the narrow sash around her waist,
        lifts the gold-threaded velvet cloak
            and lowers it over her arms,
                over her torso,
                sliding it softly
                    along her smooth sides
                till it rests about her,
                balanced on her shoulders,
    rests the silver-olive pointer hand
        suspended from her limbs,
    and places her ornamented,
        filigreed crown
            as a completion of her beauty,
                her glory.

            •

The leader takes her from you
    (you wish to hold on
    but know that would be futile;
    there are laws, commands, and rituals,
    and to depart from them

SHEKHINAH

    would hurt the one whose life,
        whose giving of life,
  is dearest to your heart)
and moves with her
          •

but in your love
    (in the blindness of your love)
you no longer see the leader,
and the scroll dances alone
    a dance of heaven, a dance of magic,
    a dance that newborns know,
    but, as they learn to walk
        like other men,
        forget,
    the dance that is the way that angels move
        in the world to come,
        the world of dreams,
    a dance of words
        that dance without words.
In silence you observe her motion
    and wish that you could comprehend
    for in her footsteps are spelled out
    all the mystic names of God.
          •

Then, murmuring (again the scattered unison)
    with all who worship in the sacred hall
        (and in Jerusalem
        and all the places that will
            someday be as one)

    you prepare for her departure
       with words of psalms:

•

"This is the generation of those
   that seek the Lord,
   who yearn for the Presence . . .
Gates, raise up your heads,
Be uplifted, ancient doors . . ."

•

We must conclude.

•

Look:
The room seems almost empty, still,
   the whispering surrounding you
      not revealing the sight of any others.

•

The Cherubim, now still as wood,
   are as if they were part
   of the ark themselves

•

and you move to join them,

•

and you touch the Ark,
   stroke its wood, its velvet
   trace the markings
   in golden-threaded braille

•

and its spirit flows into you,
   merges with you,
and in your reverie
   you become the Ark

SHEKHINAH

    become the sacred home
    wear the eternal flame
        as a signpost upon your brow
            •

and the scroll rests with you,
    rests on your shoulders,
    her ageless ancient legs relaxed,
    thighs balanced about you,
    legs draped down your chest
        like the leather straps
            of the boxes of prayers
        like the exact fringes
            of the shawl
                •

and she closes her eyes,
    calms, sleeps,
and the leader shuts the doors,
the Cherubim reassuming their initial position
            •

("She is a tree of life," they sing again,
"for those that hold her,
and those that support her
are filled with joy.")

and in the warmth, the darkness,
    the velvet holiness
    of the place you have become
           •

READING

you know that,
for the moment,
you have found peace,

that you,
and the scroll of life,
and the Presence,

are as one.

Alenu

עָלֵינוּ

Our Duty

ALENU
Our Duty

Time

•

no time

•

dark in

•

here

•

I

•

now

•

can't sense
myself

•

I am wood
solid

•

my clothing
   my lining
   velvet panels
   shreds of memory
fall away
fade away

•

SHEKHINAH

leaving
wood

•

stained by the tears of Rachel
blackened, streaked
    by the soot of the Eternal Flame
        that burns above its doors
    echoing the shards of God
        that burn,
        buried, hidden
        in husks of darkness
        in the crevices of our souls.

•

Here
the many worlds
in which we simultaneously live
are blending, blurring, running,
realities washed away
in a slurry of promises
and minimal fulfillments.

•

Jerusalem,
    if I forget—
    already the stones of the Wall
    have receded from memory
    blurring with the dull grey penciled letters
    of the wishes pressed between them.

•

The world to come
    (which has come?
    which was always here?

OUR DUTY

    Suddenly sequence shatters,
        lies in fragments,
        caught in cracked obeisance
        to the whims of omniscience
            of omnipotence
            of eternity)
    has drawn away,
    and its waters
        which had flowed with life,
        richer than blood,
        sweeter, more nourishing,
        than earthly milk or honey,
    seem no longer to be the mother flow
        of the rivers that ran
        at the heart of Eden,
    but are now a barrier,
        the rush of the currents
        now a distant clash
        of hurtling rocks
        and suspended fire.

•

This prayer hall,
    this room sanctified
    by the sacred Presence
    now seems to be—
    a room,
    and the people here are fading
    and their prayers
        sound muffled,
        hidden,
        behind a wall

SHEKHINAH

      of wood and velvet,
      silk and leather.

•

The scroll,
which had filled our senses
with its love and passion,
   its touch, its writing,
   and the sound of its words,
is now

•

simply

•

a scroll,
a careful but material assemblage
   of skins,
   inks,
   bindings and coverings,
   of tailored cloth
   and etched and hammered metals

•

The doors are closed;
the majesty, the magic
has faded.
The people outside
   this cabinet
   this casket I have become
cannot see the scroll,
cannot feel it
(in this chill of silent solitude
   I cannot even think of it
   as "her").

OUR DUTY

Without the blessings the observers
    grant to the observed
it is—

•

a scroll

•

inert weight
pressing down on my shoulders,
    bending my back,
    pushing on my arms.

•

This temporary flesh
is weaker still
than that of those
    who are always mortal.

•

We who came here,
    beckoned by song,
    summoned by prayer,
we who guided
    the Ark of the Presence
    by the waters of the world of dreams—

•

I want to go back.
I have no portion here.

•

In the distance,
    I can hear the people chant:
"A redeemer will come to Zion,

SHEKHINAH

*and to those of Jacob
who turn from willful sin."*

•

will come to Zion,
again summoned to
this world of flesh and stone

•

but only when ready
    when the redeemer is ready
    when the people are ready

•

    at the time,
    the one time,
    that all times will become.

•

Further away the people spin
    as webs form, fray, fall
    from the congregants
        to the leader
        to the scroll
        to me

•

"Holy, holy, holy . . ."
(the words dim and echo
as the leader drifts away)

•

". . . *is the Lord, Master of Legions* . . ."

•

and as the murmur of the congregants
    grows quiet
their words spread, blur, expand

into larger images,
into stranger tongues:
 •

"Holy in the most exalted heavens,
 the abode of his Presence;
Holy on earth,
 product of his strength;
Holy forever, to all eternity,
 is the Lord, Master of Legions."
 •

The heavens—abode of his Presence?
 •

She lives here,
 was just here,
 belongs among us.
 •

The leader, almost gone,
 almost disappeared,
 speaks again,
 in a voice of faded vapor:
 •

"Blessed be the Lord from his place."
 •

Again, the maddening recursiveness,
 again, the leader blesses the Blessed,
 again I wonder
  why the cycle?
  the reinforcement?
 •

SHEKHINAH

And again the response of the
    barely present congregants,
      in voices softer than the silence:

          •

"Blessed be
the honor of the Lord
from the abode of his Presence."

          •

And as dreams feed on dreams,
doubt feeds on doubt
and darkness feeds on darkness

          •

and I am alone

          •

and the Presence hides,
sequestered,
elsewhere

          •

and I look outside myself
    and I see only darkness
and I look around myself
    and everyone is gone
and I look within myself

          •

within this temporary shell

          •

and farther in,
within my soul.

          •

I know that what I sense
    is not darkness,

OUR DUTY

      not an absence of light,
      but chaos,
          emptiness,
          the murk that preceded creation,
not silence,
      but how sound sounds
      before it is sounded,
not vacuum,
      but the feeling, the lack of feeling
      in the lungs
      between breaths
      as the animal mind decides
          whether the next breath
          is to go in or out.

            •

And in this suspension
    this time beyond time
    this shadow of eternity
    that is all times that
        time has failed
        that is—
        no time

            •

I

            •

now

            •

have no framework of continuity
    no fabric to lead me

SHEKHINAH

      along its weave
    no signposts

                             •

but the prayer.

                             •

If I can tell time
    by the liturgy,
tell time
    not to stand still . . .

                           •

I call up the pages within my mind,
turn to the next prayer
I can remember.

                           •

We must stand

                         •

but I cannot feel my body,
    cannot find my feet,
        my balance,
        my will,

                     •

just the writing on the waves
    of the current of words
    that begins to travel
    through my parched soul:

                       •

*"It is our duty to praise
    the Master of all . . ."*

                    •

OUR DUTY

again blessing the Blessed,
    who can never be seen,
    whose Presence I now cannot sense
            •

". . . to give greatness to
    the Shaper of Creation . . ."
            •

again the paradox,
    as I now begin
    to flow with the words
            •

". . . for he has not made us
    like the nations of the world,
and not planted us
    like the families of the earth . . ."
            •

Not just the earth, no;
    there is a bright time, too,
    dressed as eternity,
that time which is space
    which is the energy
    which is all that matters
            •

". . . for he has not designed our destiny
    to be like theirs
nor our lot
    to be like the multitudes . . ."
            •

and we will find that time
    in that future beyond the future

SHEKHINAH

  far from the past
  within the Presence.

       •

"*...We bend our knees*
  and bow
  and acknowledge our thanks..."

       •

I cannot bow
  cannot bend my knees

       •

  for I am silent
  wood.

       •

Still I try
still I try and bow
still I try and

       •

I am falling

       •

falling

       •

down
away from heaven
down toward earth
  Its solid warming
  Its cool dark loam

       •

down

       •

and I am of the lowest of creatures
of the creatures that crawl

OUR DUTY

on the face of the earth.
I have arms but do not reach
I have legs but do not walk

I must crawl
crawl forward
wherever forward leads.
I must continue.
I know that I can crawl
and

speak

but in this darkness
this void
I have no words of my own.

Still I must continue.

And the words of the liturgy
    still flow on
proceeding through my mind
    my soul
like beckoning candles
leading me forward
    if not to a destination
    at least to a future time

And my heart reaches forward
    upward
    outward

SHEKHINAH

and grasps onto the flow of words
and pulls my mind, my soul, my life
onward in their path
     •

and I imagine God
 and imagine the Presence
and praise them
 who blessed me
 who cursed me
 who brought me here
 who planted me in temporary flesh
     •

then subtracted the world
     •

and whose images
 though they may or may not exist
pull me through this mire
 of the absence of night
     •

and I speak
 in desperation
 in pleading
 in proclamation
 in prayer
to
     •

the King who reigns over kings,
the Holy One, who is blessed,
who stretched out the heavens,
and founded the earth,
whose seat of glory is in the heavens above,

OUR DUTY

*and whose powerful Presence
   is in the loftiest heights*

•

and I crawl onward, forward

•

and the darkness is no longer
    quite so deep
and the silence is no longer
    quite so deafening
and the Presence seems no longer
    quite so far away

•

and I continue to bless the Blessed one
    that his love may yet reappear
and I pray for the touch of the Presence

•

and I continue

•

blessing the Blessed

•

and I crawl on
    crawl under
    crawl through

•

the heart of the paradox

•

blessing

•

blessing the Blessed

•

SHEKHINAH

and I enter the circuit
    the path of the process
    the oscillations
        between Creator and Created
            •

and I pray
as if I am the last person left in this world
    who knows how to pray
    who cares to pray
as if my prayer is the last strand
    binding me to our people
        our people to the Presence
        the Presence to the Lord,
            the Blessed One,
            who is Blessed
as words of ancient incantations
    spring back up into my soul
            •

for the sake of the unification
    of the Holy One, who is Blessed,
    and his Presence,
in fear and love,
to unify the Name
    in perfect unity
    in the name of all Israel
            •

and I reach forward,
    my arms becoming arms again,
    my legs becoming legs,
    my heart beginning once again
        to beat in human rhythms

OUR DUTY

    to join the pulse, the meter
    of the overtones of the heart of God
        •

and I grasp onto the words,
the words that form a healing chain
a never-ending ring of blessing
    •

and they draw me upward
  that I might stand
  and fulfill my mission
  here in this prison
    this sudden uniform
    this celebrant solidity
    this human flesh
  and that I may return
  to the land where I belong
  that I might wait
    in that time beyond time.
       •

And in the silence
  that is now merely silence
in the darkness
  that promises the light
the still voices return
  the congregants
    infinitely distant
    yet still here
  the leader
    voice transmuted
    to tones purer than music
  the Presence

SHEKHINAH

      still unseen, still unsensed
      yet comforting, warming
          as if she and I were nestled
          in each other's hearts
          in each other's arms

•

and the silence whispers:
"Do not fear the sudden terror
   or the storm that strikes the wicked . . .
   For God is with us.
Through your old age, I will remain the same;
   when you turn grey, I will endure.
I created you, and I will carry you;
   I will sustain you and save you."

•

And I stand

•

I stand

•

and speak the ancient words of praise
    the words of prayer
        that brought us to this world
    the mystic words
        in a near-forgotten language

•

in the voice of our teachers
in the voice of our leaders
in the voice of our martyrs
in the voice of our mourners
in the voice of those
    who may or may not believe

OUR DUTY

    but yet,
        if they can speak no other prayer,
        have somehow learned
            to say these words
•

blessing the Blessed
who (in the mystery of wisdom
if not the law of logic)
is, indeed, to be blessed.

Kaddish

קדיש

Mourner's Prayer

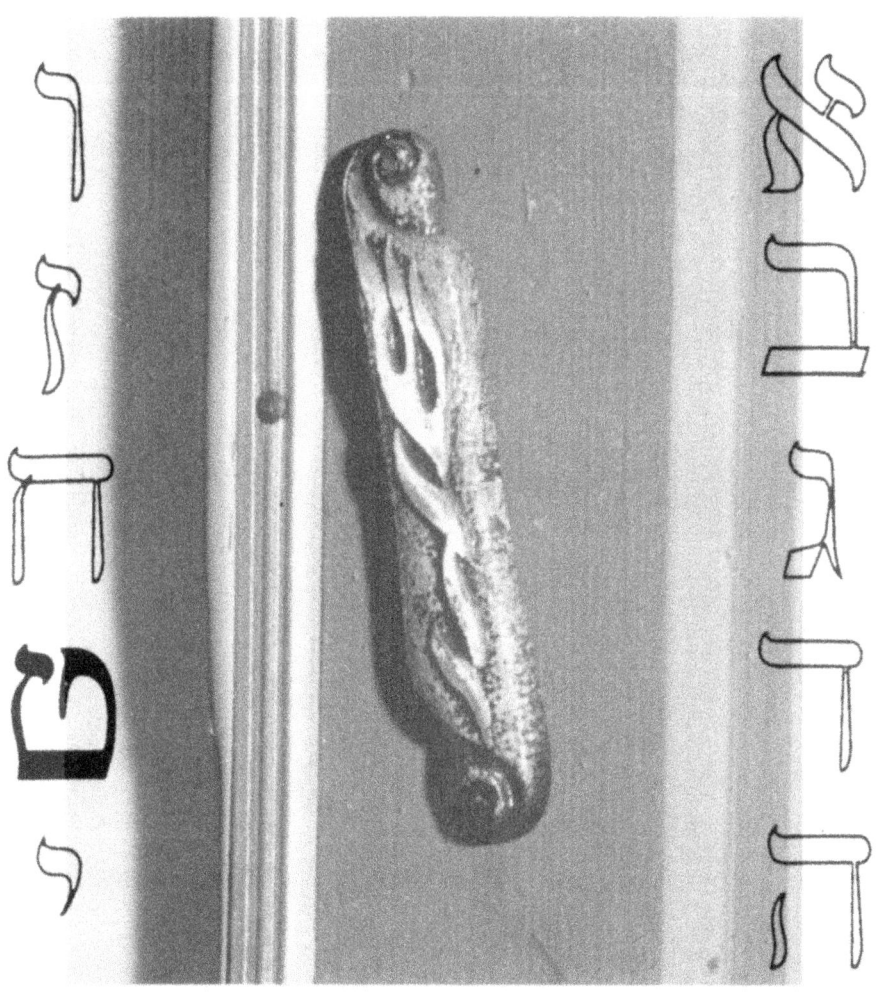

KADDISH
Mourner's Prayer

"Glorified
Sanctified
is the Great Name

     •

in the world he created
through his will.

     •

May his kingdom be established
 in your lifetimes
 in your days

     •

 in the life of the whole House of Israel
 swiftly
 soon . . .

     •

May the Great Name be blessed
forever and for all eternity;
blessed
 praised
  glorified
   exalted
    extolled
     honored
     adored
      lauded

     •

SHEKHINAH

*is the name of the Holy One, who is Blessed
beyond any blessings*
    songs
    prayers
    consolations
that are ever spoken in this world.
        •

*May there be abundant peace in heaven
and life for us
and for all Israel.*
        •

*The Maker of Peace in the heavens
will make peace for us
and for all Israel . . ."*
        •

The service now is ending.
        •

It's time to go home now.
        •

The child's ark
    the ark you guided into this flood of realities
    the ark of your own private
        Covenant with the Presence
is waiting.
        •

Follow the leader.
Lie down upon the waters of time.
Lie down to pass beyond the pillars,
    beyond the guardian rivers
    of rock and fire.
Lie down to travel

MOURNER'S PRAYER

    at right angles to the flow of sleep,
    the six words of peaceful proclamation
        hovering in the slow breath
        that forms above your silent lips.

•

With a kiss of the spirit,
    a touch of her hand,
    the Presence leads you onward

•

    she who, though she seems invisible,
        is always by your side.

•

The sounds of the psalms of the seven days
    echo and blend within your heart.
The readings of the scroll of the law
    for all weeks
    for all years
    surround you, enfold you.

•

For you, all times are the same again,
    all space collapsed
        to a point within your soul,

•

and the voice of the leader,
and the power of the Presence,
guide you

•

(step
pause
step)

•

SHEKHINAH

away.

Hosafot
הוספות
Beyond Conclusions

HOSAFOT
Beyond Conclusion

In hushes close to silence
the prayers dissolve, transmute.

•

Those who follow minority traditions
continue, reading psalms
    commandments
    structures of principles
    a daily page of learning
together, apart,
    in pairs, in silence

•

Others,
prayers finished for the morning,
prepare to leave.

•

The murmur of the congregants
slowly shifts
    from the magical to the mundane
    from sacred texts to software systems
    from Bible study to business plans.

•

There is no prayer
    to mark the end of prayer,
no verbal separation between

SHEKHINAH

    the sacred and the secular.
Worshippers reach for the velvet bags
placed earlier on the shelf
                •

and gradually remove from themselves
    the boxes of prayers
    the leather straps
    the prayer shawls,
        black and white and blue,
        fringes of white and blue.
                •

But the sense of the Presence
the holiness of the articles
    in which the congregants
    have clothed themselves to pray
is not removed;
                •

a coating of the sacred
stays with each soul,
to be preserved,
    enhanced, or
    dissipated
by the actions of the day.
                •

Listen now:
    the last of the prayers is complete,
    the sounds of the service replaced by
        traffic
        banter

telephone calls.
This hall of prayer is now again

•

a room

•

with sacred books
and the Ark, with its scrolls within,

•

mute,
yet bearing silent testimony
to the purpose that they will
once again
serve.

•

Look now,
touch the textures of the wooden
    walls
    seats
    floors,
inhale,
taste,

•

the air of this room,
    now mundane
    but retaining some strange sacredness,

•

feel,
with senses that have no human name,
the Presence

•

SHEKHINAH

who waits forever in this hall
who looks down from heaven
    and ahead and back
    at ancestors and children
    across the plains of space
    along the rivers of time
who follows those who move within
    this apparently real world.
                  •

The leather straps unwind
    unspelling the Holy Name
    encrypted in their twists.
(No golem now could be enlivened
    by these items
    as they lie, dark, inert,
    within their cases;
a human touch must warm them,
    give them form, before
    any sacred power can
    course along their lines.)
The prayer shawls fold,
    in half,
    quarters,
    then in eighths,
gently, solemnly, like honored flags,
and join the others in their cases.
                    •

It's time to go home now.
              •

BEYOND CONCLUSION

Yet the Presence reaches out once more
all moments crystallized within her gaze.
•
Invisible, in silence,
she moves along,
around the time-encrusted congregants,
to grace the hall, the walls, the doorways
through which all who leave must pass.
•
One final kiss, then,
for those who leave
 to greet the warmth of morning.
Her spirit fills the box of memories
 that stands sentry
  on the doorposts of the hall.
•
One kiss then,
 as she stands there
 in her gentle light.
Sister to the scrolls,
 she touches lips to hands,
 as those who pass her
 have touched theirs to theirs,
then touches hands to loving hands
•
and her fingers whisper messages
to the listening palms
of those who sense her there:
•
I am with you now, forever,
 as you venture out,

SHEKHINAH

    into the harsher rush of morning.
I have always been with you,
    in righteousness and justice,
        kindness, mercy,
    with you who knew of me and loved me,
    even with each of you
        who may or may not have known
            that I was there,
        who may or may not have cared,
           have listened,
           have believed.
I will always be with you,
    in faithfulness,
    and you will know my love
    as you wander onward
        through this world,
    as you pass beyond this life
        to the unknown,
    as you, within the mist, await the day

•

    that all times will again be one,
    that all of space will come together,
    that the river of life will flow
        beyond the pillars
        beyond the walls between the worlds
    and what was once the Earth
        will be once again a garden
        and all pain will be forever banished
        and all people will be clothed
        in the flesh of truth and honest love
    and all will eat without shame

    of the firm, sweet fruit of life
    digesting the knowledge of good and evil
and the serpents
    will again walk proudly,
    will walk straight-legged, tall and wise,
and all creatures
    will discover their true names
        as whispered in their ears by Adam
        but forgotten for an endless moment
        when first the garden was concealed.

•

I am with you,
was,
will be with you
in all my hidden forms:

•

Rachel,
    tears about to turn to joy
    at the transformation of her children

•

the Sacred Scrolls,
    the ink and parchment gaining life
    and dancing free, a skin of comfort

•

the Moon,
    her cycles shown to be
    illusions framed by the tides of Earth,
    forever full, forever shining,
    with glory equal to the sun

•

SHEKHINAH

the Sabbath,
    Queen of Comfort, mystic day
    that all days will soon become.
                       •

Listen:
    the daughter of a voice
    you hear within
    as you catch your breath
        before you say
        each one of your passing prayers
    is the modulation
        the harmony
        of my voice with your own.
                      •

Listen:
                      •
    Here till the end of days
                      •
    we together as one
                      •
    now
                      •
    stand.
                      •

Listen:
                      •
    I will be with you,
    remaining here in my hall to dream
    as in my dreams I enter yours
        and guide you onward
                      •

BEYOND CONCLUSION

through the world of life
through the world of dreams
through the greater world

•

within your souls.

Afterword and Bibliography

Afterword

The area of Jewish mysticism in general, and of the Shekhinah in particular, is broad and complicated; aspects of the beliefs evolved and expanded over time, often creating contradictory branches. It would be impossible to give a proper history and explanation of the figure here.

I hope that the bibliography which follows this note will help those who have read this to look further into these areas.

Although I had a strong Jewish education, I don't recall the figure of the Shekhinah being mentioned at all in my training. The first reference to it that I saw was in *The Divine Invasion*, a science fiction novel by Philip K. Dick, which, however, included no pointers to further information.

In 1989, soon after I moved to Austin, I met several followers of contemporary Paganism, and, intrigued by their beliefs and rituals, began investigating goddess imagery in various religions. In the course of the search, I found the article "Encountering the Shekhinah" by Rabbi Leah Novick in Shirley Nicholson's anthology *The Goddess Reawakening*. That article pointed me back to my own Jewish background, and led me to the research from which I wrote this piece.

In May, 1990, I began composing *Shekhinah* as a scenario for a dance/theatre piece. In the fall of that year, one of the dancers that I was hoping to recruit asked me to write a fuller explanation of the basis of the text. That

SHEKHINAH

explanation quickly turned into an early version of this poem. The poem was also designed to work as a text for the performance. Since it is so long, the performance uses a condensed version which is about half the length.

This project would not have been possible without the help of many other people. Among them:

Cheryl Solis and Claudia Crowley, the book's editors;

The Information Development Team at Analysts International Corporation's Corporate Support Facility in Austin;

Rabbi Leah Novick, who criticized an early version of the text;

Deborah Hay and Beverly Bajema, who encouraged me to pursue the dance performance, and in whose workshops we developed the piece;

The Human Systems performance group (Jan Barstow, Manu Bird, Jana Stevens, Nicholas Schriber, and Kip Garth);

Mark Hillis of Morgan Printing, H.J.J. Hewitt, Matthew Sharlot, and Eureka Purity, who helped in the production of the book;

Temple Beth Israel of Austin, the B'nai Brith Hillel Foundation at the University of Texas, and the Austin Chabad House for their help in the photography.

Mary Owen, Sheilah Murthy, Ann Zbylot, ML Winter, Jeff Wilson, Tim Bigham, Bob Izenberg, John Jansen, Natalie Maul, Linda Cast, Lance Spangler, Paul Bodin, Jennifer V. Haefele, Christi Bone, Chris Kelly, and all the others who helped in equally essential though less identifiable ways.

Bibliography

Birnbaum, Philip, translator and editor. *Daily Prayer Book*. New York: Hebrew Publishing Company, 1977.

Green, Arthur. "Bride, Spouse, Daughter: Images of the Feminine in Classical Jewish Sources." In *On Being a Jewish Feminist,* edited by Susannah Heschel. New York: Schocken, 1983.

Hoffman, Edward. *The Way of Splendor: Jewish Mysticism and Modern Psychology*. Boulder, CO: Shambhala, 1981.

Idel, Moshe. *Kabbalah: New Perspectives*. New Haven: Yale University Press, 1988.

Matt, Daniel Chanan, translator and editor. *Zohar: The Book of Enlightenment*. Ramsey, NJ: Paulist Press, 1983.

Nachman of Breslov. *Rabbi Nachman's Tikkun*. Edited and translated by Abraham Greenbaum. New York: Breslov Research Institute, 1984.

Novick, Leah. "Encountering the Shekhinah." In *The Goddess Reawakening*, compiled by Shirley Nicholson. Wheaton, IL: Quest Books/The Theosophical Publishing House, 1989.

Ochs, Carol. *Beyond the Sex of God: Toward a New Consciousness Transcending Matriarchy and Patriarchy*. Boston: Beacon Press, 1977.

Patai, Raphael. *The Hebrew Goddess.* New York: Avon, 1991.

Plaskow, Judith. *Standing Again at Sinai.* New York: HarperCollins, 1990.

Schochet, Jacob Immanuel. *Mystical Concepts in Chassidism.* Brooklyn: Kehot Publication Society, 1981.

Scholem, Gershom. *Kabbalah.* New York: New American Library, 1974.

— *Major Trends in Jewish Mysticism.* New York: Schocken, 1961.

— *On the Mystical Shape of the Godhead: Basic Concepts in the Kabbalah.* Translated by Joachim Neugroschel and edited by Jonathan Chipman. New York: Schocken, 1991.

— *Origins of the Kaballah.* Translated by Allen Arkush and edited by R. J. Werblowsky. Princeton: Princeton University Press, 1987.

Sherman, Nosson, translator and editor. *The Complete Artscroll Siddur.* New York: Artscroll, 1984.

Shneuer Zalman of Liadi. *Likutei Amarim (Tanya).* Translated by Nissan Mindel. Brooklyn: Kehot Publication Society, 1981.

Tanakh: A New Translation of the Holy Scriptures According to the Traditional Hebrew Text. Philadelphia: Jewish Publication Society, 1985.

Trachtenberg, Joshua. *Jewish Magic and Superstition: A Study in Folk Religion.* New York: Atheneum, 1939.

www.ingramcontent.com/pod-product-compliance
Lightning Source LLC
Chambersburg PA
CBHW032358040426
42451CB00006B/55